A Classic
CHRISTMAS
CAROLING
Songbook

30 Sing-Along ❧ Favorites ❧

The classic carols of Christmas carry the joy of the season from year to year—especially when shared in the company of others. With words and music from *The Christian Life Hymnal*, these 30 carols were selected for their richness of message and timeless appeal. Whether you're standing on a snowy porch with friends, gathered around a piano with family, visiting the lonely, or worshiping in a small group, may they help you spread the light of Christmas in song.

Angels from the Realms of Glory

1

1. An - gels from the realms of glo - ry, wing your flight o'er
2. Shep - herds in the field a - bid - ing, watch - ing o'er your
3. Sag - es, leave your con - tem - pla - tions, bright - er vi - sions
4. Saints, be - fore the al - tar bend - ing, watch - ing long in
5. Though an in - fant now we view Him, He shall fill His

all the earth; ye who sang cre - a - tion's sto - ry,
flocks by night, God with us is now re - sid - ing;
beam a - far; seek the great De - sire of Na - tions;
hope and fear; sud - den - ly the Lord, de - scend - ing,
Fa - ther's throne, gath - er all the na - tions to Him;

Refrain

now pro - claim Mes - si - ah's birth:
yon - der shines the in - fant Light:
ye have seen His na - tal star: Come and wor - ship,
in His tem - ple shall ap - pear.
ev - ery knee shall then bow down.

come and wor - ship, wor - ship Christ, the new - born King.

WORDS: James Montgomery, 1816; st. 5, *The Christmas Box*, 1825
MUSIC: *Regent Square*, Henry Thomas Smart, 1867

8.7.8.7 with Refrain

Angels We Have Heard on High

2

1. An - gels we have heard on high sweet - ly sing - ing o'er the plains,
2. Shep - herds, why this ju - bi - lee? Why your joy - ous strains pro - long?
3. Come to Beth - le - hem and see Him whose birth the an - gels sing;
4. See Him in a man - ger laid, whom the choirs of an - gels praise;

and the moun-tains in re - ply ech - o - ing their joy - ous strains.
What the glad-some ti - dings be which in-spire your heaven-ly song?
come, a - dore on bend-ed knee Christ the Lord, the new-born King.
Ma - ry, Jo - seph, lend your aid, while our hearts in love we raise.

Refrain

Glo - - - - ri - a,

in ex - cel - sis De - o! Glo -

- - ri - a, in ex - cel - sis De - o!

WORDS: French carol, tr. James Chadwick, 1862
MUSIC: *Gloria,* French carol, 18th c.

7.7.7.7 with Refrain

Away in a Manger

1. A - way in a man - ger, no crib for a bed, the lit - tle Lord Je - sus laid down His sweet head; the stars in the bright sky looked down where He lay, the lit - tle Lord Je - sus, a - sleep on the hay.

2. The cat - tle are low - ing, the poor Ba - by wakes, but lit - tle Lord Je - sus, no cry - ing He makes; I love Thee, Lord Je - sus! Look down from the sky, and stay by my cra - dle till morn - ing is nigh.

3. Be near me, Lord Je - sus, I ask Thee to stay close by me for - ev - er, and love me, I pray; bless all the dear chil - dren in Thy ten - der care, and fit us for heav - en, to live with Thee there.

WORDS: st. 1-2, traditional carol; st. 3 attr. John Thomas McFarland, ca. 1906
MUSIC: *Away in a Manger*, James Ramsey Murray, 1887

11.11.11.11

4 Away in a Manger

1. A - way in a man - ger, no crib for a bed, the lit - tle Lord Je - sus laid down His sweet head; the stars in the bright sky looked down where He lay, the lit - tle Lord Je - sus, a - sleep on the hay.

2. The cat - tle are low - ing, the poor Ba - by wakes, but lit - tle Lord Je - sus, no cry - ing He makes; I love Thee, Lord Je - sus! Look down from the sky, and stay by my cra - dle till morn - ing is nigh.

3. Be near me, Lord Je - sus, I ask Thee to stay close by me for - ev - er, and love me, I pray; bless all the dear chil - dren in Thy ten - der care, and fit us for heav - en, to live with Thee there.

WORDS: st. 1-2, traditional carol; st. 3 attr. John Thomas McFarland, ca. 1906
MUSIC: *Cradle Song*, William James Kirkpatrick, 1895

11.11.11.11

Come, Thou Long-Expected Jesus

1. Come, Thou long - ex - pect - ed Je - sus, born to set Thy
2. Born Thy peo - ple to de - liv - er, born a Child, and

peo - ple free; from our fears and sins re - lease us;
yet a King, born to reign in us for - ev - er,

let us find our rest in Thee. Is - rael's strength and
now Thy gra - cious king - dom bring. By Thine own e -

con - so - la - tion, hope of all the earth Thou art; dear de -
ter - nal Spir - it, rule in all our hearts a - lone; by Thine

sire of ev - ery na - tion, joy of ev - ery long - ing heart.
all - suf - fi - cient mer - it, raise us to Thy glor - ious throne.

WORDS: Charles Wesley, 1744
MUSIC: *Hyfrydol*, Rowland Hugh Pritchard, ca. 1830; harm. *The English Hymnal*, 1906

8.7.8.7 D

6 Ding! Dong! Merrily on High

1. Ding! Dong! Mer-ri-ly on high in heaven the bells are ring-ing.
2. E'en so here be-low be-low let stee-ple bells be swung-en,
3. Pray you, du-ti-ful-ly prime Your mat-in chime, ye ring-ers;

Ding! Dong! Ve-ri-ly the sky is rent with an-gel sing-ing.
And "i-o,* i-o, i-o," by priest and peo-ple sung-en.
may ye beau-ti-ful-ly rhyme your eve-time song, ye sing-ers.

Refrain

Glo - - - - ri-a, ho-san-na in ex-cel-sis!

Latin for hurrah!

WORDS: G.R. Woodward, early 20th c.
MUSIC: *Ding Dong Merrily*, 16th c. French melody, harm. Charles Wood, 1926

7.7.7.7 with Refrain

Go, Tell It on the Mountain

Refrain
Unison

Go, tell it on the moun - tain, o - ver the hills and ev-ery-where;

go, tell it on the moun - tain that Je - sus Christ is born!

Harmony

1. While shep-herds kept their watch-ing o'er si - lent flocks by night, be -
2. The shep-herds feared and trem-bled when, lo! a - bove the earth rang
3. Down in a low - ly man - ger the hum - ble Christ was born, and
4. — When I was a seek - er, I sought both night and day; I

hold, through-out the heav-ens there shone a ho - ly light.
out the an - gel cho - rus that hailed our Sav - ior's birth.
God sent us sal - va - tion that bless - ed Christ-mas morn.
asked the Lord to help me, and He showed me the way.

WORDS: Negro spiritual, 19th c. adapt. John Work, Jr., 1907
MUSIC: *Go Tell It*, Negro spiritual, 19th c.

7.6.7.6 with Refrain

8 God Rest Ye Merry, Gentlemen

1. God rest you merry, gen-tle-men, let noth-ing you dis-
2. From God our heaven-ly Fa - ther, a bless-ed an - gel
3. "Fear not," then said the an - gel, "let noth-ing you af-
4. The shep-herds at those ti - dings re - joic-ed much in
5. But when to Beth - le - hem they came, where - at this in - fant
6. Now to the Lord sing prais - es all you with - in this

may, re - mem-ber Christ, our Sa - vior was born on Christ-mas
came, and un - to cer - tain shep - herds brought tid-ings of the
fright; this day is born a Sav - ior of a pure vir - gin
mind, and left their flocks a - feed - ing in temp-est, storm and
lay, they found Him in a man - ger where ox - en feed on
place, and with true love and char - i - ty each oth - er now em-

day, to save us all from Sa - tan's power when we were gone a - stray:
same; how that in Beth - le - hem was born the Son of God by name.
bright, to free all those who trust in Him from Sa-tan's power and might."
wind, and went to Beth-l'em straight - way this bless-ed Babe to find.
hay, His Mo-ther Ma - ry, kneel - ing un - to the Lord did pray.
brace. This ho - ly tide of Christ - mas doth bring re-deem-ing grace.

Refrain

O tid - ings of com - fort and joy, com-fort and

joy, O tid - ings of com - fort and joy!

WORDS: English traditional, 19th c.
MUSIC: English carol, 19th c.; arr. John Stainer, 1871

Irregular

Good Christian Friends, Rejoice

1. Good Chris-tian friends, re-joice with heart and soul and voice; give ye heed to what we say: Je - sus Christ is born to-day; ox and ass be - fore Him bow, and He is in the man-ger now. Christ is born to-day! Christ is born to - day!

2. Good Chris-tian friends, re-joice with heart and soul and voice; now ye hear of end-less bliss; Je - sus Christ was born for this! He has o - pened heav - en's door, and we are blest for-ev - er-more. Christ was born for this! Christ was born for this!

3. Good Chris-tian friends, re-joice with heart and soul and voice; now ye need not fear the grave: Je - sus Christ was born to save! Calls you one and calls you all to gain His ev - er-last - ing hall. Christ was born to save! Christ was born to save!

WORDS: Latin carol, 14th c.; tr. John Mason Neale, 1853, alt.
MUSIC: *In Dulci Jubilo*, German, 14th c.

Irregular

10 Good King Wenceslas

1. Good King Wen-ces-las looked out on the feast of Ste-phen,
2. "Hi-ther, page, and stand by me, if you know it, tell-ing,
3. "Bring me drink and bring me meat, bring me pine logs hith-er,
4. "Sire, the night is dark-er now, and the wind blows strong-er,
5. In his ma-ster's steps he trod, where the snow lay dint-ed;

when the snow lay round a-bout, deep and crisp and e-ven;
yon-der pea-sant, who is he? Where and what his dwell-ing?"
you and I will see him eat, when we bear them thith-er."
fails my heart, I know not how; I can go no long-er."
heat was in the ve-ry sod which the saint had print-ed.

bright-ly shone the moon that night, though the frost was cru-el,
"Sire, he lives a good league hence, un-der-neath the moun-tain,
Page and mon-arch, forth they went, forth they went to-geth-er,
"Mark my foot-steps, my good page, tread now in them bold-ly,
There-fore, Chris-tians all be sure, wealth or rank pos-sess-ing,

when a poor man came in sight, gath-ering win-ter fu-el.
right a-gainst the for-est fence, by Saint Ag-nes' foun-tain."
through the cold wind's wild la-ment and the bit-ter weath-er.
you shall find the win-ter's rage freeze thy-self less cold-ly."
you who now will bless the poor shall your-selves find bless-ing.

WORDS: John Mason Neale, 1853, alt.
MUSIC: *Tempus Adest Floridum,* from *Piae Cantiones,* 1582; arr. John Stainer

7.6.7.6 D

Hark! The Herald Angels Sing

1. Hark! The her - ald an - gels sing, "Glo - ry to the new - born King;
2. Christ, by high - est heaven a - dored; Christ, the ev - er - last - ing Lord!
3. Hail the heaven-born Prince of Peace! Hail the Sun of Right-eous-ness!

peace on earth, and mer - cy mild, God and sin - ners rec - on - ciled!"
Late in time be - hold Him come, off - spring of the Vir - gin's womb.
Light and life to all He brings, risen with heal - ing in His wings.

Joy - ful, all ye na - tions, rise, join the tri - umph of the skies;
Veiled in flesh the God-head see; hail th'in - car - nate De - i - ty,
Mild He lays His glo - ry by, born that man no more may die,

with th'an - gel - ic host pro-claim, "Christ is born in Beth - le - hem!"
pleased with us in flesh to dwell, Je - sus, our Em - man - u - el.
born to raise the sons of earth, born to give them sec - ond birth.

Refrain

Hark! The her-ald an - gels sing, "Glo - ry to the new - born King."

WORDS: Charles Wesley, 1739; alt. George Whitefield, 1753, and others
MUSIC: *Mendelssohn*, Felix Mendelssohn, 1840; arr. William Hayman Cummings, 1856   7.7.7.7 D with Refrain

12
In the Bleak Midwinter

WORDS: Christina Georgina Rossetti, 1872
MUSIC: *Cranham,* Gustav Theodore Holst, 1906

Irregular

It Came upon the Midnight Clear

1. It came up-on the mid-night clear, that glor-ious song of old,
2. Still through the clo - ven skies they come with peace-ful wings un-furled,
3. Yet with the woes of sin and strife the world has suf-fered long;
4. O ye, be-neath life's crush-ing load whose forms are bend-ing low,
5. For lo! The days are hasten-ing on, by pro-phets seen of old,

from an-gels bend-ing near the earth to touch their harps of gold:
and still their heaven-ly mu - sic floats o'er all the wea - ry world;
be - neath the heaven-ly hymn have rolled two thou-sand years of wrong;
who toil a - long the climb-ing way with pain-ful steps and slow;
when with the ev - er - cir - cling years shall come the time fore-told,

"Peace on the earth, good-will to men, from heaven's all gra-cious King."
a - bove its sad and low-ly plains they bend on hover-ing wing,
and war-ring hu - man-kind hears not the ti - dings which they bring;
look now, for glad and gol - den hours come swift-ly on the wing:
when the new heaven and earth shall own the Prince of Peace their King,

The world in sol - emn still-ness lay to hear the an - gels sing.
and ev - er o'er its Ba - bel-sounds the bless-ed an - gels sing.
O hush the noise and cease your strife and hear the an - gels sing!
O rest be-side the wea - ry road, and hear the an - gels sing.
and all the world send back the song which now the an - gels sing.

WORDS: Edmund Hamilton Sears, 1850
MUSIC: *Carol*, Richard Storrs Willis, 1849

CMD

14

Joy to the World!

1. Joy to the world! The Lord is come: let earth re - ceive her
2. Joy to the earth! The Sav - ior reigns: let all their songs em -
3. No more let sins and sor - rows grow, nor thorns in - fest the
4. He rules the world with truth and grace, and makes the na - tions

King; let ev - ery heart pre - pare Him room,
ploy; while fields and floods, rocks, hills, and plains
ground; He comes to make His bless - ings flow
prove the glo - ries of His righ - teous - ness

and heav'n and na - ture sing, and heaven and na - ture
re - peat the sound - ing joy, re - peat the sound - ing
far as the curse is found, far as the curse is
and won - ders of His love, and won - ders of His

1. and heav'n and na - ture sing,

1. and heav'n and na - ture sing, and

sing, and heav'n, and heav'n and na - ture sing.
joy, re - peat, re - peat the sound - ing joy.
found, far as, far as the curse is found.
love, and won - ders, won - ders of His love.

heav'n and na ture sing,

WORDS: Isaac Watts, 1719, alt.; para. Psalm 98
MUSIC: *Antioch,* attr. Charles Rider, n.d.;
   William Holford, 1834, adapt. Lowell Mason, 1836

CM with Repeats

Lo, How a Rose E'er Blooming

1. Lo, how a Rose e'er bloom-ing from ten - der stem hath
2. I - sa - iah 'twas fore - told it, the Rose I have in
3. The shep - herds heard the sto - ry pro - claimed by an - gels
4. This flower, whose fra - grance ten - der with sweet - ness fills the

sprung, of Jes - se's lin - eage com - ing, as those of old have
mind; with Mar - y we be - hold it, the Vir - gin Moth - er
bright, how Christ, the Lord of glo - ry was born on earth this
air, dis - pel in glo-rious splen-dor the dark-ness ev - ery-

sung. It came, a blos-som bright, a - mid the cold of
kind. To show God's love a - right, she bore to us a
night. To Beth - le - hem they sped and in the man - ger
where. True man, yet ver - y God, from sin and death He

win - ter, when half - spent was the night.
Sav - ior, when half - spent was the night.
found Him, as an - gel her - alds said.
saves us and light - ens ev - 'ry load.

WORDS: German carol, 16th c.; tr. Theodore Baker, 1897
MUSIC: *Eis Ist Ein Ros'*, from *Geistliche Kirchengesäng*, 1599; tr. Michael Praetorius, 1609

7.6.7.6.6.7.6

16 Love Came Down at Christmas

1. Love came down at Christ - mas, love all love - ly,
2. Wor - ship we the God - head, love in - carn - ate,
3. Love shall be our to - ken; love be yours and

love di - vine; love was born at Christ - mas,
love di - vine; wor - ship we our Je - sus:
love be mine, love to God and neigh - bor

star and an - gels gave the sign.
but where-with for sa - cred sign?
love for plea and gift and sign.

WORDS: Christina Georgina Rossetti, 1885, alt.
MUSIC: *Garton*, traditional Irish melody

6.7.6.7

17 O Come, All Ye Faithful

1. O come, all ye faith - ful, joy - ful and tri - um - phant, O
2. God of God, Light from Light e - ter - nal,
3. Child, for us sin - ners, poor and in the man - ger,
4. Sing, choirs of an - gels, sing in ex - ul - ta - tion, O
5. Yea, Lord, we greet Thee, born this hap - py morn - ing,
6. Lo! Star - led chief - tains, ma - gi, Christ a - dor - ing,

come, ye, O come ye to Beth - le - hem! Come and be-
Lo! He ab - hors not the Vir - gin's womb; Ve - ry
we would em - brace Thee with love and awe; who would not
sing, all ye cit - i - zens of heaven a - bove! Glo - ry to
Je - sus to Thee be all glo - ry given; Word of the
of - fer Him frank-in-cense and gold and myrrh; we to the

hold Him, born the King of an - gels!
God, be - got - ten, not cre - a - ted;
love Thee, lov - ing us so dear - ly?
God, all glo - ry in the high - est!
Fa - ther, now in flesh ap - pear - ing!
Christ - child bring our hearts ob - la - tions;

Refrain

O come, let us a - dore Him, O come, let us a - dore Him,

O come, let us a - dore Him, Christ the Lord!

WORDS: John Francis Wade, c. 1743; tr. Frederick Oakley, 1841, and others
MUSIC: *Adeste Fideles,* John Francis Wade, ca. 1743;
    harm. from *Collections of Motetts or Antiphons,* 1792

Irregular with Refrain

18

O Come, Little Children

1. O come, lit - tle chil - dren, O come, one and all, to Beth - le - hem haste, to the man - ger so small; God's Son for a gift has been sent you this night to be your Re - deem - er, your joy, and de - light.

2. He's born in a sta - ble for you and for me, draw near by the bright gleam - ing star - light to see, in swad - dling clothes ly - ing so meek and so mild, and pur - er than an - gels, the heav - en - ly Child.

3. See Ma - ry and Jo - seph, with love - beam - ing eyes, are gaz - ing up - on the rude bed where He lies; the shep - herds are kneel - ing, with hearts full of love, while an - gels sing loud Hal - le - lu - jahs a - bove.

4. Kneel down and a - dore Him with shep - herds to - day, lift up lit - tle hands now and praise Him as they; re - joice that a Sav - ior from sin you can boast, and join in the song of the heav - en - ly host.

5. Dear Christ Child, what gifts can we chil - dren be - stow by which our af - fec - tion and glad - ness to show? No rich - es and trea - sures of val - ue can be, but hearts that be - lieve are ac - cept - ed with Thee.

WORDS: Christian von Schmid, ca. 1840
MUSIC: *O Come, Little Children*, Johann Abraham Peter Schultz, 18th c.

11.11.11.11

O Come, O Come, Emmanuel

*1. O come, O come, Emmanuel, and ransom captive
2. O come, Thou Wisdom from on high, Who orderest all things
3. O come, Thou Rod of Jesse, free Thine own from Satan's
*4. O come, Thou Day-spring, come and cheer our spirits by Thine
5. O come, Thou Key of David, come, and open wide our
6. O come, O come, great Lord of might, who to Thy tribes on
*7. O come, Desire of nations, bind in one the hearts of

Israel that mourns in lonely exile here, un-
mightily; to us the path of knowledge show, and
tyranny; from depths of hell Thy people save and
advent here; and drive away the shades of night, and
heavenly home; make safe the way that leads on high, and
Sinai's height in ancient times once gave the law in
all mankind; bid thou our sad divisions cease, and

Refrain

til the Son of God appear.
teach us in her ways to go.
give them victory o'er the grave.
pierce the clouds and bring us light!
close the path to misery.
cloud and majesty and awe.
be Thyself our King of Peace

Rejoice! Re-

joice! Emmanuel shall come to thee, O Israel.

*Note: Stanzas 1, 4 and 7 are included on the Split Track Compact Disc companion recording.
WORDS: Latin, 12th c.; tr. John Mason Neale, 1851; Henry Sloan Coffin, 1916; and others
MUSIC: *Veni Emmanuel*, 15th c. plainsong; adapt. Thomas Helmore, 1854

L.M. with Refrain

20

O Holy Night!

1. O ho - ly night! The stars are bright - ly shin -
2. Led by the light of faith se - rene - ly beam -
3. Tru - ly He taught us to love one an - oth -

ing, it is the night of the dear Sav - ior's birth!
ing, with glow - ing hearts by His cra - dle we stand.
er; His law is love and His gos - pel is peace;

Long lay the world in sin and er - ror pin - ing, till He ap -
So led by light of a star sweet - ly gleam - ing, here came the
chains shall He break, for the slave is our broth - er, and in His

peared and the soul felt its worth. A thrill of
wise men from O - ri - ent land. The King of
name all op - pres - sion shall cease. Sweet hymns of

WORDS: Placide Cappeau, 1855; tr. John Sullivan Dwight
MUSIC: *Cantique De Noel*, Adolphe-Charles Adams, 1847

Irregular

21 · O Little Town of Bethlehem

1. O lit-tle town of Beth-le-hem, how still we see thee lie!
2. For Christ is born of Ma - ry; and gath-ered all a - bove,
3. How si - lent - ly, how si - lent - ly the won-drous gift is giv'n!
4. Where chil-dren pure and hap - py pray to the Bless-ed Child,
5. O ho - ly Child of Beth-le-hem, de - scend to us, we pray;

A - bove thy deep and dream-less sleep the si - lent stars go by;
while mor-tals sleep, the an - gels keep their watch of won-dering love.
So God im-parts to hu - man hearts the bless-ings of His heav'n.
where mis - er - y cries out to Thee, Son of the Moth - er mild;
cast out our sin, and en - ter in, be born in us to - day.

yet in thy dark streets shin - eth the ev - er - last - ing Light;
O morn-ing stars to - geth - er, pro - claim the ho - ly birth!
No ear may hear His com - ing, but in this world of sin,
where char - i - ty stands watch-ing and faith holds wide the door,
We hear the Christ-mas an - gels, the great glad ti - dings tell;

the hopes and fears of all the years are met in Thee to - night.
and prais - es sing to God the King, and peace to all on earth
where meek souls will re - ceive Him still the dear Christ en - ters in.
the dark night wakes, the glo - ry breaks, and Christ-mas comes once more.
O come to us, a - bide with us, our Lord, Em - man - u - el!

WORDS: Phillips Brooks, 1868
MUSIC: *St. Louis*, Lewis Henry Redner, 1868

C.M.D.

O Little Town of Bethlehem

22

1. O lit-tle town of Beth-le-hem, how still we see thee lie!
2. For Christ is born of Ma - ry; and gath-ered all a - bove,
3. How si - lent-ly, how si - lent-ly the won-drous gift is giv'n!
4. Where chil-dren pure and hap - py pray to the bless-ed Child,
5. O ho - ly Child of Beth-le - hem, de-scend to us, we pray;

A - bove thy deep and dream-less sleep the si - lent stars go by;
while mor-tals sleep, the an - gels keep their watch of wond'ring love.
So God im-parts to hu - man hearts the bless-ings of His heav'n.
where mis-er - y cries out to Thee, Son of the Moth-er mild;
cast out our sin, and en - ter in, be born in us to - day.

yet in thy dark streets shin - eth the ev - er - last-ing Light;
O morn-ing stars to - geth - er, pro-claim the ho - ly birth!
No ear may hear His com - ing, but in this world of sin,
where char - i - ty stands watch - ing and faith holds wide the door,
We hear the Christ-mas an - gels, the great glad ti - dings tell;

the hopes and fears of all the years are met in Thee to - night.
and prais - es sing to God the King, and peace to all on earth.
where meek souls will re - ceive Him still the dear Christ en - ters in.
the dark night wakes, the glo - ry breaks, and Christ-mas comes once more.
O come to us, a - bide with us, our Lord, Em - man - u - el!

WORDS: Phillips Brooks, 1868
MUSIC: *Forest Green*, English melody; adapt. Ralph Vaughn Williams, 1906

C.M.D.

23 Once in Royal David's City

1. Once in roy-al Da-vid's cit-y stood a lowly cat-tle shed, where a Moth-er laid her Ba-by in a man-ger for His bed; Ma-ry was that Moth-er mild, Je-sus Christ her lit-tle Child.

2. He came down to earth from heav-en, Who is God and Lord of all, and His shel-ter was a sta-ble, and His cra-dle was a stall; with the poor, and mean, and low-ly lived on earth our Sav-ior ho-ly.

3. And, through all His won-drous child-hood, He would hon-or and o-bey, love and watch the low-ly Maid-en in whose gen-tle arms He lay; Christ-ian chil-dren all should be kind, o-bed-ient, good as He.

4. For He is our child-hood's pat-tern, day by day like us He grew; He was lit-tle, weak and help-less, tears and smiles like us He knew; and He feel-eth for our sad-ness, and He shar-eth in our glad-ness.

5. And our eyes at last shall see Him, through His own re-deem-ing love; for that Child so dear and gen-tle, is our Lord in heav'n a-bove, and He leads His chil-dren on to the place where He is gone.

6. Not in that poor low-ly sta-ble, with the ox-en stand-ing by, we shall see Him; but in heav-en, set at God's right hand on high; when like stars His chil-dren crowned, all in white shall wait a-round.

WORDS: Cecil Frances Alexander, 1848
MUSIC: Irby, Henry John Gauntlett, 1849; harm. A.H. Mann, 1919

8.7.8.7.7.7

Silent Night!

WORDS: Joseph Mohr, 1816; trans. John Freeman Young, 1863
MUSIC: *Stille Nacht*, Franz Xaver-Grüber, 1818

Irregular

25

The First Noel

1. The first No - el the an - gel did say was to cer-tain poor shep-herds in fields as they lay; in fields where they lay keep-ing their sheep, on a cold win-ter's night that was so deep.
2. They look - ed up and saw a star shin-ing in the east, be - yond them far, and to the earth it gave great light, and so it con - tin - ued both day and night.
3. And by the light of that same star three wise men came from coun - try far; to seek for a king was their in - tent, and to fol - low the star wher - ev - er it went.
4. Then let us all with one ac - cord sing prais - es to our heaven - ly Lord; that hath made heaven and earth of naught, and with His blood man - kind hath bought.

Now - ell, Now - ell, Now - ell, Now - ell, born is the King of Is - ra - el.

*In this carol, Nowell (Latin novellae) means news, and Noel (Latin natalis) means birthday.
WORDS: English Carol, 19th c.
MUSIC: The First Nowell, 19th c., English Carol; arr. John Stainer, 1871

Irregular

Unto Us Is Born a Son

1. Un - to us is born a Son, King of choirs su -
2. Christ, from heaven de - scend - ing low, comes on earth a
3. This did He - rod sore af - fray, and griev - ous - ly be -
4. Of His love and mer - cy mild this the Christ - mas
5. A and O and O and A, cum can - ti - bus in
* Al - pha and O - me - ga He, Sing we now to -

per - nal: see on earth His life be - gun, of lords the Lord e -
strang - er; ox and ass their own - er know, be - cra - dled in the
wild - er, so he gave the word to slay, and slew the lit - tle
sto - ry; O that Ma - ry's gen - tle Child might lead us up to
cho - ro, let our mer - ry or - gan go. Be - ne - di - ca - mus
geth - er, let our mer - ry or - gan go. O bless the Lord for

ter - nal, of lords the Lord e - ter - nal.
man - ger, be - cra - dled in the man - ger.
chil - der, and slew the lit - tle chil - der.
glo - ry, might lead us up to glo - ry.
Do - mi - no, be - ne - di - ca - mus Dom - i - no.
ev - er, O bless the Lord for ev - er.

*optional translated stanza

WORDS: Latin, from *The Moosburg Gradual*, ca. 1360; st. 1-5, tr. George Ratcliffe Woodward, 1910;
st. 5 alternate wording tr. Eric Wyse, 2005
MUSIC: *Puer nobis nascitur*, melody from *Piae Cantiones*, harm. Eric Wyse, 2005
7.6.7.7.7
© 2005 Vine Ridge Music BMI (administered by ICG)

27 We Three Kings of Orient Are

1. We three kings of O - ri - ent are, bear - ing
2. Born a King on Beth - le - hem's plain, gold we
3. Frank - in - cense to of - fer have I, in - cense
4. Myrrh is mine, its bit - ter per - fume Breathes a
5. Glor - 'ous now be - hold Him a - rise, King and

gifts we trav - erse a - far, field and foun - tain, moor and moun - tain,
bring to crown Him a - gain, King for - ev - er, ceas - ing nev - er
owns a De - i - ty nigh; prayer and prais - ing, all men rais - ing,
life of gath - er - ing gloom; Sor - r'wing, sigh - ing, bleed - ing, dy - ing,
God and Sac - ri - fice; Al - le - lu - ia! Al - le - lu - ia!

fol - low - ing yon - der star.
o - ver us all to reign.
wor - ship Him, God on high. O
Sealed in the stone - cold tomb.
Sounds through the earth and skies.

star of won - der,

star of night, star with roy - al beau - ty bright, west - ward lead - ing,

still pro - ceed - ing, guide us to thy per - fect light.

WORDS: John Henry Hopkins, 1857
MUSIC: *Kings of Orient*, John Henry Hopkins, 1857

8.8.8.6. with Refrain

We Wish You a Merry Christmas

28

1. We wish you a mer-ry Christ-mas, we
2. We sing you this Christ-mas bless-ing, great
3. May God's grace and peace be with you, may

wish you a mer-ry Christ-mas, we wish you a mer-ry
joy now we are con-fess-ing; best wish-es to you ad-
God's grace and peace be with you, may God's grace and peace be

Christ-mas, and a hap-py New Year! Glad tid-ings we bring to
dress-ing for a hap-py New Year!
with you through-out the New Year!

you, and your kin, glad tid-ings for Christ-mas, and a hap-py New Year!

WORDS: traditional English carol; st. 2 and 3, Danny Jones, Eric Wyse, 2005
MUSIC: *We Wish You a Merry Christmas,* traditional English carol
© 2005 Vine Ridge Music BMI (admin. by ICG)

Irregular with Refrain

29

What Child Is This?

1. What Child is this, who, laid to rest, on Ma-ry's lap is sleep - ing, whom an-gels greet with an-thems sweet, while shep-herds watch are keep - ing? This, this is Christ the King, whom shep-herds guard and an-gels sing. Haste, haste to bring Him laud, the Babe, the Son of Ma-ry!

2. Why lies He in such mean es - tate where ox and ass are feed - ing? Good Christ-ians, fear, for sin-ners here the si - lent Word is plead - ing. Nails, spear shall pierce Him through, the cross be borne for me, for you. Joy, joy for Christ is born, the Babe, the Son of Ma-ry!

3. So bring Him in - cense, gold and myrrh, come, peas-ant, king, to own Him. The King of kings sal-va-tion brings, let lov - ing hearts en-throne Him. Raise, raise the song on high; the Vir - gin sings her lul - la - by. Joy, joy, for Christ is born,

This tune may be sung in the original dorian mode by sharping all C's in the melody and alto parts (keeping the bass in measures 3 and 11 unaltered.)

WORDS: William C. Dix, ca. 1865
MUSIC: *Greensleeves*, traditional English melody, 16th c.; harm. John Stainer, 1821, alt.

8.7.8.7 with Refrain

While Shepherds Watched Their Flocks

30

1. While shep-herds watched their flocks by night, all seat-ed on the ground, the an-gel of the Lord came down and glo-ry shone a-round, and glo-ry shone a-round.
2. "Fear not," he said (for might-y dread had seized their trou-bled mind); "glad tid-ings of great joy I bring to you and all man-kind, to you and all man-kind."
3. "To you, in Dav-id's town this day is born of Dav-id's line a Sav-ior, who is Christ the Lord, and this shall be the sign: and this shall be a sign:"
4. "The heav'n-ly Babe you there shall find to hu-man view dis-played all mean-ly wrapped in swad-dling bands, and in a man-ger laid, and in a man-ger laid."
5. Thus spake the ser-aph, and forth-with ap-peared a shin-ing throng of an-gels prais-ing God, who thus ad-dressed their joy-ful song: ad-dressed their joy-ful song;
6. "All glo-ry be to God on high, and to the earth be peace: good will to all from high-est heav'n be-gin and nev-er cease, be-gin and nev-er cease!"

WORDS: Nahum Tate, 1700
MUSIC: *Christmas*, George Frederic Handel, from an air in *Siroe*, 1728; arr. Lowell Mason, 1821   C.M. with Repeat